The Bard & Scheherazade Keep Company

THE BARD
&
SCHEHERAZADE

Keep Company

BY
Jan D. Hodge

ABLE MUSE PRESS

First published in 2017 by

Able Muse Press

www.ablemusepress.com

Printed in the United States of America

Library of Congress Control Number: 2017930335

ISBN 978-1-927409-85-5 (paperback)
ISBN 978-1-927409-84-8 (digital)

Cover image: "Shades of Dramatics" by Alexander Pepple

Cover & book design by Alexander Pepple

Able Muse Press is an imprint of *Able Muse:* A Review of Poetry, Prose & Art—at www.ablemuse.com

Able Muse Press
467 Saratoga Avenue #602
San Jose, CA 95129

For Bruce and Barbara Bedell
and those many friends who have enjoyed these over the years

Acknowledgments

"The Taming of the Shrew" first appeared in *Umbrella*,

"The Ass" in *Off the Coast*,

"The Invitation to Universal Peace" in *American Arts Quarterly*,

and

"The Tale of the First Captain" in *Lavender Review*.

Contents

Acknowledgments   vi

I. THE BARD   1

    Romeo and Juliet   3
    The Taming of the Shrew   4
    Richard III   6
    A Midsummer Night's Dream   8
    The Merchant of Venice   10
    I Henry IV   13
    Much Ado About Nothing   15
    Julius Caesar   18
    As You Like It   20
    Hamlet   24
    Twelfth Night   27
    King Lear   29
    Measure for Measure   31
    Macbeth   33
    Antony and Cleopatra   35
    The Tempest   37

II. SCHEHERAZADE   41

    The Tale of the Second Kalandar   43
    The Ass   54
    The Historic Fart   57
    The Tale of the Leg of Mutton   61
    The Invitation to Universal Peace   68
    The Tale of the First Captain   72

III. REYNARD THE FOX   81

    Reynard the Fox   83

Notes   99

I. THE BARD

Romeo and Juliet

Saddest of tragedies—
Juliet Capulet
tumbles in love with fair
Romeo's grace,
but to her sorrow an
irreconcilable
family quarrel pre-
cludes their embrace.

Troublesome circumstance!
Romeo Montague,
killing her kinsman in
combat of arms,
finds himself threatened with
prosecutorial
action and flees from his
Juliet's charms.

Frantic and woebegone,
Romeo's Juliet,
hopelessly hoping her
lover to keep,
gets from her chaplain a
pharmacological
tincture that brings on a
death-aping sleep.

Rushing to be with her,
Juliet's Romeo
swallows a poison, be-
lieving her dead.
Waking, she—pitiful
epithalamion!—
joins him in death on that
sorrowful bed.

The Taming of the Shrew

The story's familiar:[1]
a blackguard in search of
a fortune is courting
an ill-tempered shrew
whose father deplores her
anathematizing
behavior towards all who
might otherwise woo.

Her sister Bianca
has too many suitors
to count, but her father
will not let her wed
until, he remonstrates
reiteratively,
his Katherine is married
and taken to bed.

Petruchio senses
much more than a fortune
and sets out to win her
despite her repute,
for he is convinced the
denunciatory
reports are uncalled-for—
and she is a beaut!

He holds up a mirror
reflecting her actions,
denying her dresses
and food and repose,
apparently acting
vituperatively;
but it isn't brutal,
it's right on the nose—

1. Okay, so it's amphibrachs. So are "Hamlet" and "Antony and Cleopatra."

a strategy rooted
in fondness, and proving
more winning than when she
was humored and bribed,
and when she discerns his
uxoriophilic
intent, it is just what
the doctor prescribed.

She finds her true selfhood
in loving and serving
a husband who dotes on
a spirited wife,
since, rightly considered,
propitiatory
behavior's a sauce to
the gusto of life.

Forget all that fuss of
Bianca, her suitors,
her father's frustration,
and even the gold,
for they are the keenest
demystification
of well-suited lovers
we'll ever behold.

The husbands' last wager
provides us a further
and fitting reversal
confirming this view;
the contest makes clear the
identification
we'd always suspected—
Bianca's the shrew.

Richard III

Last of the Yorkist line,
Richard Plantagenet
climbed to the throne on a
mountain of dead.
Humpbacked, he plotted with
Machiavellian
gusto; his motto was
"Off with his head!"

Tewksbury witnessed his
slaughter of Edward, whose
widow thereafter he
took to his bed.
Anyone faulting such
insensitivity
should've known better; 'twas
"Off with his head!"

He had his brother and
then his two nephews all
killed in the Tower, or
so it is said.
Hastings and Stanley, who
ideologically
balked at his crowning, heard
"Off with his head!"

All the queen's kinsmen and
then his "friend" Buckingham
felt the keen edge as his
treachery spread—
prodigal intra- and
extrafamilial
killings to encores of
"Off with his head!"

Finally England would
brook no more tyranny.
Faced with rebellion, to
Bosworth he fled,
where (overtaken by
thanatophobia)
wanting a horse, he would
lose his *own* head!

————

Students of Clio[2] may
raise their objections to
such a portrayal as
false and absurd.
We merely shrug at the
historiographers,
happily taking the
Bard at his word.

2. The Muse of
history.

A Midsummer Night's Dream

Now the occasion of
Theseus' wedding to
lovely Hippolyta
signals our theme:
how lovers' whimsical
irrationalities
joyously romp in a
summer night's dream.

Come to the forest where
four young Athenians
(Hermia, Helena,
and their two beaus)
try to discover a
non-acrimonious
way of resolving their
various woes.

Fairy King Oberon
dislikes Titania's new
love for a foundling, and
so out of spite
tells Puck to fetch him an
aphrodisiacal
flower to vanquish that
rival delight.

Then he arranges to
help the young lovers, but
Puck messes up and the
wrong guy is juiced.
Pity poor Helena!
Uncomprehendingly,
now she is grievously
doubly misused.

Meanwhile a motley of
well-meaning citizens,
gathered to practice a
tragical skit,
prove to be players most
unsatisfactory—
much too much bumbling and
too little wit.

Oberon, learning that
Puck inadvertently
crossed up the lovers, mis-
taking his guy,
has him make up for his
imperspicaciousness,
righting the pairings he'd
twisted awry.

Cleverly, Puck plays a
trick of his own, so that
willful Titania, a-
sleep in the grass,
wakes to a wonderful
implausibility—
falling for Bottom, turned
into an ass.

This being comedy,
all is resolved and the
nuptials proceed. May the
newlyweds fare
better than Thisbe and
tatterdemalion
Pyramus, victims of
death and despair.

The Merchant of Venice

So that Bassanio
might woo his Portia, the
merchant Antonio,
good man and true,
borrows on hazard and
unprecedentedly
pledges his flesh unto
Shylock the Jew.

Grateful, Bassanio
hastens to Belmont where
suitors of Portia must
venture their skill,
for she is bound by the
inelasticity
set by the terms of her
late father's will.

Choosing a casket—will
silver or gold or less
fanciful lead be the
key to delight?—
serves as the test of their
eligibility.
Haply, Bassanio
chooses aright.

Meanwhile, Lorenzo has
run off with Jessica,
wanting to marry the
Jew's only child.
Shylock, informed of her
tergiversational
conduct, cries out he's been
robbed and defiled.

News that Antonio's
ships have miscarried has
made him default on his
debt to the Jew.
Flush with resentment and
intractability,
Shylock insists on the
flesh as his due.

Portia, disguised as a
barrister, argues for
mercy, not malice, but
he is unmoved,
stating that justice will
incontrovertibly
sanction an action the
law has approved.

Then, after noting the
bond doesn't warrant the
taking of blood as he
sharpens his knife,
she introduces a
counterhypothesis:
since he's imperiled a
citizen's life,

he stands in forfeit of
life and estate. But the
Duke and Antonio
wisely forbear
if he'll relinquish his
heterodoxical
faith and entitle his
daughter as heir.

("Jew dog" and "usurer,"
cursing his daughter for
loving a Christian, yet
does he not feel?
How do we balance a
stereotypical
villain against a man
painfully real?)

Then off to Belmont, where
after some awkwardness
over some rings that were
given away,
romance prevails with the
temperamentally
well suited lovers and
closes the play.

I Henry IV

Rebels are challenging
Bolingbroke's dubious
claim to the kingdom as
Henry the Fourth—
Owen Glendower the
genethlialogist,
Douglas the Scot, and the
Percys up north.

Hal's at the Boar's Head in
Eastcheap carousing with
Falstaff, which surely puts
grace to the test—
Falstaff, that dissolute
Pantagruelian
liar compulsively
given to jest.

Henry would fain have a
son more like Hotspur, de-
fiant and proud, but a
man to the bone,
rather than hear of such
unmeritorious
conduct disgracing the
heir to the throne.

Hal, though, is politic,
sounding the people and
skillfully playacting
various parts;
under the obvious
censurability
of his behavior, he's
winning their hearts.

Armed with authority,
Falstaff abuses it,
pressing to service a
pitiful crew.
Hotspur, impulsive and
irreconcilably
nursing hostility,
burns for a coup.

Hal meets and vanquishes
Hotspur in combat and
rescues his father from
Douglas's sword,
ending all doubt of his
honorability.
Peace is established and
order restored.

———

In the play's sequels, the
dying king finally
blesses the son he had
oft viewed askance.
Hal, newly crowned, after
unsentimentally
casting off Falstaff, wins
glory in France.

Much Ado About Nothing

Benedick—bachelor,
scorner of women—darts
arrows at Beatrice,
setting the tone.
She meets his risible
egocentricity
with a superlative
wit of her own.

Claudio, smitten, asks
Pedro as proxy to
court lovely Hero and
win her consent.
John throws a damnable
discontinuity
into the wooing to
wreck their intent.

Friends delude Benedick
into believing that
Beatrice loves him and
suffers apart,
then hint to Beatrice
axiomatically
she is the mistress of
Benedick's heart.

Drunken Borachio
boasts of John's villainy:
Hero was wrongfully
"proven" unchaste.
Dogberry's lexical
dysfunctionality
turns this, however, to
nonsense posthaste.

So the disclosure is
badly delayed, and poor
Hero's denounced when she
thought to be wed.
Reeling from Claudio's
unceremonious
censure, she faints, and is
bruited as dead.

Beatrice swears she is
blameless, and Benedick
guesses that John is the
cause of the slur.
Checking their quick-witted
idiosyncrasies,
she admits loving him,
he loving her.

Beatrice, banking on
newfound devotion (for
they'd been remarkably
tractable dupes,
quickly forgetting his
gametophobia),
asks him to kill his friend
Claudio. Oops!

Benedick offers the
challenge, but Claudio
finally learns of the
treacherous ruse;
shamed by the fatal ir-
revocability
of his aspersion, he
pales at the news.

He to atone will pay
homage to Hero, and
marry her cousin (her
father's request),
only to witness an
impossibility:
Hero's alive! And their
marriage is blest.

Writing bad sonnets and
bantering giddily,
Benedick also proves
ready to wed,
laughing off jibes he'll be
unrecognizable
wearing a yoke and with
horns on his head.

Julius Caesar

Cassius and Casca eye
Caesar's ascendancy
jealously. Hoping to
cut it off short,
yet keep their treachery
uncontroversial,
they persuade Brutus to
lend his support.

Caesar, advised that the
omens are sinister,
scoffs at Calpurnia's
plea to stay home.
He can't be bothered with
negligibilities
meant to embarrass a
pillar of Rome.

Reaching the Capitol,
Caesar is stabbed by the
several conspirators,
acting, they claim,
solely to foster a
nondictatorial
Roman Republic. So
where is the blame?

Brutus lets Antony
speak at the funeral of
Caesar, and working the
crowd with finesse,
he tells them Brutus sees
megalomania
rather than virtue in
Caesar's success.

How ineffective the
voices of reason and
honor when one can so
easily play
on the mob's recreant
malleability!
Riot let loose drives the
traitors away.

Brutus and Cassius fall
out over ethics, but
friendship is stronger for
good or for ill.
Brutus then learns by his
extracorporeal
presence that Caesar is
powerful still.

Antony's forces and
those of Octavius,
gathered at Philippi,
can't be ignored;
sensing a fatal in-
exorability,
Cassius, then Brutus, each
falls on his sword.

Antony knows that of
all the conspirators
Brutus alone bore no
personal shame;
he alone acted not
unpatriotically,
nor out of envy of
Caesar's acclaim.

As You Like It

As the play opens, the
good Duke's in exile, and
Frederick holds sway with a
self-serving creed,
decency's bountiful
intrinsicality
rudely uprooted by
malice and greed.

Likewise, Orlando, his
birthright sucked dry by his
envious brother,[3] is
forced to depart,
having won over (not
coincidentally)
Charles the wrestler and
Rosalind's heart.

Rosalind, banished as
well, heads for Arden in
search of her father, the
Duke as it were.
Celia, given the
perdurability
of their relationship,
journeys with her.

Arden: the Duke and his
courtiers encounter a
natural world free of
flattery's bane,
though it is never quite
overidealized;
winter is brutal and
poverty strain.

3. I.e., Oliver.

20

Outcast Orlando finds
welcome among them, and
Rosalind too, though dis-
guised as a youth.
There she meets Silvius,
unqualifiably
pining for Phebe, but
thwarted forsooth.

Corin and Touchstone make
light of his passion, but
Rosalind knows that his
anguish is dire.
She views the shepherd not
unsympathetically,
feeling the same about
her heart's desire.

Meanwhile, Orlando is
papering Arden with
verses dashed off in a
passional fit—
fodder for Jaques's
antipoetical
diatribes laced with his
cynical wit.

Finding herself so ex-
tolled in his rhymes, how can
Rosalind (Ganymede)
tease him with tact?
Mocking his postures, she
unprepossessingly
offers to teach him how
lovers should act.

She, seeing Phebe still
scorning poor Silvius,
chastises her for un-
warranted pride.
Haply, though, Phebe has
(misapprehendingly)
fallen for . . . Ganymede!
What shall betide?

Oliver, saved from a
lion, surrenders his
right to Orlando, to
Celia his heart.
Ganymede's game in its
inauthenticity
wearies Orlando, dis-
pleased with his part.

Touchstone half fancies the
pastoral idyll and,
taken with Audrey as
nature decreed,
tries to prevail on the
extraparochial
Oliver Martext to
sanction the deed.

Still unresolved is the
frustrating, troublesome
knot of Orlando's and
Phebe's despair.
Rosalind, kenning its
explicability,
promises soon to un-
tangle the snare.

When she abandons her
guise as young Ganymede,
showing Orlando her
heart fond and true,
he is transported, and
complementarily
Phebe takes Silvius,
loving anew.

Frederick's decided to
give up the dukedom and
enter a life of re-
ligious retreat.
Right is restored and so
(anticlimactically)
farewell to Arden. Our
story's complete.

Hamlet

Prince Hamlet's uneasy;
he's met with a spectre
that told him his father
was wickedly slain.
Or was the appearance
hallucinatory,
a trick of ill humor
that fevered his brain?

But if it were true (and
Horatio bore witness),
momentous the burden
the fact would entail,
for duty demanded
retaliatory
dispatch of the villain
to balance the scale.

But murder his uncle?
He's married his mother—
is Denmark's new king. What
a spot to be in!
He sits here, head hanging,
deliberatively
deploring his plight and
adrift in chagrin.

He well understands his
precarious footing—
his need to proceed as
forbearance admits,
and mocking a manic
personification,
plays games of intrigue with
a couple of twits.

Some actors appearing,
he seizes the chance to
pursue his objective
by using their play,
adapting the script and
theatricalizing
the murder to catch out
his uncle. Touché!

The king, feeling guilty,
asks God for forgiveness,
but vainly—though Hamlet,
observing him there,
in spite of his clearly
incriminatory
behavior refuses
to slay him at prayer.

Yet chastising mama,
he haply discovers
Polonius spying—
a nasty surprise—
and recklessly stabs him.
(Expostulatory
intruders are apt to
meet such a demise.)

Laertes returns to
avenge his dead father
and finds his dear sister
half out of her mind,
her life in all senses
deteriorating:
her father's been killed and
her lover's unkind.

Laertes spots Hamlet
and they exchange words at
the grave of Ophelia
(who drowned in a brook),
though he and the king have
collaboratively
made plans to kill Hamlet
by hook or by crook:

a challenge to swordplay,
a poisoned épée and
a death-dealing draught to
make sure of the deed.
(We have here a perfect
exemplification
of amoral statecraft
made lawful by need.)

The fencers each suffer
a wound that proves mortal,
the queen drains the chalice,
the king gets his due—
a terrible price for
ameliorating
that rottenness which had
made Denmark a slough.

With Claudius, Gertrude,
Laertes, and Hamlet
all dead in this rush of
coagulate gore,
the state will effect the
legitimitizing
of Fortinbras, named to
bring order once more.

Twelfth Night

Viola, shipwrecked and
fearing her brother has
perished, disguises her-
self as a youth.
Meanwhile, Orsino loves
melodramatically
playing the lover, but
loves he in truth?

Lovelorn, the duke sends his
"youth" to Olivia,
wooing by proxy. Her
own heart astir,
she does his bidding but
involuntarily.
Mercy! Olivia's
fallen for her!

Faced with this exquisite
impracticality—
he loving she loving
"he" loving he—
Viola greets it with
unflappability,
charmingly witty and
blithe as can be.

Toby and Aguecheek
carry on raucously
(Toby is fleecing poor
Andrew for sport)
when, with his Puritan
hedonophobia,
killjoy Malvolio
brings them up short.

Scorning the upstart, the
revelers scheme so that
he will mistakenly
think he is loved.
Biting, the jackanapes
seriocomically
flirts with his mistress, cross-
gartered and gloved.[4]

4. So I fudged.
   "Yellow-
   stockinged"
   wouldn't fit.

Aguecheek, sensing his
courtship is foolish, is
prodded to challenge his
rival to fight.
Taken aback by this
pusillanimity,
Viola flees from the
fainthearted knight.

Seeking a rematch, the
cowardly Andrew runs
into . . . Sebastian! who
hadn't been drowned.
That explains, given the
verisimilitude,
why hapless Andrew gets
thoroughly crowned.

Viola tenders her
hand to Orsino, her
twin having taken the
countess's heart;
what a connubial
amicability—
save for Malvolio,
sulking apart.

King Lear

Lear, king of Albion,
acting imprudently,
parcels his kingdom by
posing a test:
who's to get what will be
idiopathically
settled according to
who loves him best.

Honest Cordelia, who
chafes at the spectacle,
vows that she loves him, but
no more than due.
Sensing a slight in such
ungenerosity,
Lear casts her off with a
graceless adieu.

Regan and Goneril,
vain and falsehearted,
flatter their father, then
drive him from home—
scorn and disparage him
uncompromisingly,
leave him to quake in the
storm with Poor Tom.

Meanwhile, the dastardly
Edmund, the offspring of
Gloucester's old lechery,
hatches a plan:
calling on Nature, he
opportunistically
gammons poor Edgar and
cons his old man.

What has become of the
banished Cordelia,
loving her father though
married to France?
Taken and hanged in the
geopolitical
warfare with Edmund by
fatal mischance.

Trustworthy Kent and the
good Duke of Albany
stand by the king, who is
broken by grief.
Sinned against far beyond
sufferability,
Lear finds in dying his
only relief.

———————

Many years afterward,
Nahum Tate, Laureate,
finding this tragedy
grievously drear,
softened its terrible
unbearability,
saving Cordelia and
comforting Lear.

Measure for Measure

Angelo's charged by the
Duke of Vienna with
clearing the brothels that
sully the town,
he himself having a
nonconfrontational
nature, but knowing they
must be pulled down.

Angelo orders to
prison one Claudio,
guilty of getting his
truelove with child.
Proud in his puritan
impassability,
he couldn't possibly
be so beguiled.

When Isabella comes
pleading for Claudio,
Angelo finds himself
shaken by lust.
Having so jeopardized
creditability,
does he still merit the
general trust?

Angelo offers to
pardon her brother if
she'll play the wanton, a
double-edged knife;
bound for the cloister, she
unaltruistically
values her chastity
more than his life.

Claudio, though, is not
willing to die, so the
Duke (now disguised as a
man of the cloth),
knowing that Angelo's
illiberality
led him to break off a
previous troth,

fashions a plan to have
unwary Angelo
bed Marianne[5] at a
trysting instead.
Angelo, far from con-
ciliatorily,
still demands reprobate
Claudio's head.

When Isabella de-
nounces him publicly,
Marianne tells of his
dissolute lie.
Faced with his profligate
irregularities,
first he must honor his
troth—and then die.

Both of the women beg
mercy for Angelo,
Claudio's life has been
spared by a fluke,
and (yet it hardly seems
rationalizable)
staunch Isabella will
marry the Duke.

5. I.e., Mariana,
his former
betrothed. If I
alter her name,
Shakespeare did
so with Isabella's
when metrically
apt ("Isabel," II, iv,
4; III, i, 147; IV,
iii, 107; V, i, 437,
etc.).

Macbeth

What have the witches to
say to Macbeth, who seems
eager to know what his
future may bring?
Awed by their mystical
ineffability,
he hears them prophesy
he will be king.

Lady Macbeth, when she's
told of the prophecy,
fears that her husband lacks
heart to proceed,
so with ferocious in-
domitability
urges him on to a
damnable deed.

Driven by visions of
daggers and blood, he can
not turn aside from the
storm in his breast.
Mad with ambition, he
irreverentially
murders a kinsman, his
king and his guest.

He is then haunted by
hyperacusia;
voices accosting him
fill him with dread.
Knocking awakens the
unmagisterial
porter, but can't rouse the
king from his bed.

Banquo is murdered, but
comes as a ghost to the
banquet, a guest such as
conscience might bring.
Clearly, despite all the
paraphernalia,
febrile Macbeth is ill-
suited as king.

Shaken, he visits the
Sisters, suspecting the
blood that he wades in will
not be enough,
then with a merciless
execrability
slaughters the children and
wife of Macduff.

Malcolm engages an
army in England and
marches to Scotland to
unseat Macbeth.
Meanwhile, undone by a
neurodegenerate
madness, his queen meets an
untimely death.

Hearing that Birnam Wood
marches to Dunsinane,
jaded Macbeth knows that
he will be slain—
killed by Macduff, as the
uncontradictable
Sisters portended—and
Malcolm will reign.

Antony and Cleopatra

The world in the offing,
Octavius Caesar
and Antony vie for
ascendence in Rome.
But Tony prefers the
barbarianism
of soft beds in Egypt
to duties at home.

The death of his wife and
political chaos
bring Antony home to
address what's amiss,
and there he accepts the
conciliatory
arrangement of wedding
Octavius' sis.

But Tony loves Cleo
and so, disregarding
both rumors that paint him
with shameful repute
and Caesar's attempt at
disorientation,
he heads back to Egypt—
with Rome in pursuit.

At Actium Tony
is winning the battle
when he is abruptly
betrayed by his queen.
He dotingly gives up
imperialistic
ambitions and meekly
abandons the scene.

They quarrel, and Cleo,
to win back his favor,
sends word that, despairing,
she's done herself in.
Defeated, and scorning
capitulatory
behavior, he plays the
true Roman again.

But death arrives slowly
and Cleo still lives, so
he's brought to her tower
where ill fortune spurs
a lofty and poignant
reunification;
he dies in her arms, and
the last act is hers.

Rejecting her role as
a war prize of Caesar,
the queen takes an asp to
her bosom to flout
his insolent views of
colonialism.
Defiance in death lends
a noble way out.

The Tempest

Prospero, exiled from
Milan[6] with only his
daughter (as duke he'd been
less than astute),
lives on an unpeopled
Mediterranean
island he shares with a
sprite and a brute.

Ariel, freed from the
witchwork of Sycorax,
gladlier waits upon
Prospero's will;
Caliban, compound of
implacabilities,
uses his tongue but to
curse and speak ill.

Magically Prospero
causes a shipwreck, which
brings his old enemies
into his reach,
where he with wisdom and
equitability
sets about visiting
justice on each.

First he brings Ferdinand,
son of the king, to his
daughter Miranda, and
happily, lo!
mutual rapture, an
extemporaneous
waking to love in a
maid and her beau.

6. Yep, the Bard
pronounced it
MILL-un; see
I, ii, 54–5; II, i,
112–14; V, i, 205;
etc.

Meanwhile, Antonio
urges Sebastian to
rise up and murder his
brother the king.
Ariel guards the king's
vulnerability,
wakening him to his
conscience's sting.

Ferdinand passes the
trial set by Prospero,
winning Miranda, and,
moved by delight,
Prospero conjures a
semidiaphanous
pageant to honor their
nuptial rite.

Sack-addled, Caliban
schemes with Stephano to
wrest back his island from
Prospero's rule,
till his new hero's in-
satiability—
lusting for fripperies!—
proves him a fool.

Reason prevails over
fury, and Prospero
pardons Alonso, sets
Ariel free,
and, having seen how his
bibliomania
led to distress, drowns his
book in the sea.

As he reclaims his old
dukedom in Milan, a
world for Miranda so
brave and so new,
he, although pleased by her
anthropophilia,
holds to his rather more
politic view.

II. SCHEHERAZADE

The Tale of the Second Kalandar

Then said Scheherazade, I will tell you the tale told by the second poor kalandar[7] of how he came to be blind:

> I am a king and the
> son of a king, and a
> once renowned master of
> science and art,
> known for the graceful in-
> comparability
> of my calligraphy,
> dear to my heart.

> Summoned to Hind,[8] I set
> sail with a shipload of
> gifts, but was driven to
> shore by a squall,
> where I fell victim to
> inopportunity:
> dust storms and robbers de-
> prived me of all.

> Wounded, I fled to a
> glittering city, where
> haply a tailor took
> pity on me
> (praise to Allah!), for my
> knowledgeability
> weighed in the marketplace
> less than a flea.

7. A Sufi mystic or holy man.

8. Hindustan (i.e., India).

With his assistance, I
worked for a year as a
woodcutter. Then, on a
morning in spring,
as I was chopping an
unmusicality
rang in my ear. I had
struck a brass ring.

Straining, I lifted and
saw a great staircase that,
drawing me down, all my
senses a-whirl,
led to a fabulous
infraterranean
palace where languished a
beautiful girl.

"Are you a man or a
djinn?" she entreated. "A
man, I assure you." "Who
led you to me?"
"Who but Allah!" And her
demonophobia
being thus answered, I
listened as she

told me her story: how
twenty years since, on the
night of her wedding, an
evil ifrit
carried her off and had
unmitigatedly
kept her confined in that
cheerless retreat.

"Every ten days he comes
here to possess me, but
you needn't fear; for the
next several nights
we can be sure this in-
variability
leaves us occasion for
wanton delights."

Five or six days we had
pleasured in love and in
music and wine when I
urged with a kiss:
"I am a master of
cacodemonia.
Trust me, my love, I will
free you from this."

"No. Be content with the
pleasure I promise you—
nine nights in ten; that is
surely enough."
Giddy with rapture and
rodomontadery,
I didn't listen, but
stomped in a huff.

"You have destroyed me, for
Jurjis[9] is on to you.
Did I not warn you? Now
flee if you can!"
In a rare moment of
inequanimity,
I, like the whelp of a
guttersnipe, ran.

9. The ifrit, "true
seed of the Evil
One."

45

But I'd forgotten my
axe, and returning, I
gazed on a fiend only
hell could have bred.
Hideous, panting with
semiarticulate
fury, he seized my poor
darling. I fled.

Quickly concealing the
door to the staircase, I
made my way back to the
tailor in shame,
hating myself for my
imperspicaciously
acting in ways that would
blacken my name.

Shortly thereafter, the
tailor approached me and
said that a Persian was
asking for me.
Sensing a fearful in-
evitability
in my adventure, I
knew it was . . . *he.*

Then the earth opened, and
Jurjis erupted—my
knees turned to water, my
backbone to wax—
and with horrific and
incontrovertible
insolence hissed at me:
"This is your axe!"

Next thing I knew, he had
seized me and carried me
back to that palace where
she had been mine.
No! I was shocked into
insensibility,
seeing her ravaged by
cruel design!

"Here is your lover, you
unfaithful sow." And he
passed her a scimitar.
"Strike off his head!"
She stood unmoving, but
self-sacrificingly
disavowed knowing me.
Jurjis saw red.

Glaring at me, he roared:
"*You* cut off *her* head." "But
I have no knowledge that
she has done wrong.
I can do nothing so
heterodoxically
heinous." She winked, for my
reason was strong.

Jurjis exploded: "That
wink is your death!" And he
struck with the scimitar
hard on her nape.
"You, dog, shall suffer an
ultrasophisticate's
curse!" And I found myself
turned to an ape.

So he bewitched me, and
how I arrived on that
desolate mountain I
don't understand,
but with a firm inde-
fatigability
week after fortnight I
wandered the land,

railing at fate, till I
(praise to Allah!) was in
sight of the sea and a
ship in the bay.
Here was my chance, and my
incomprehensible
feeling of helplessness
melted away.

Nimbly I raced up the
rigging, but sailors were
shouting, "The beast is an
omen of ill!
Kill him!" A dizzying
disequilibrium
caused me to fall, and they
closed for the kill.

Moved by my weeping, the
captain took pity, and
fortune was finally
smiling on me,
offering opportune
subequatorial
passage to Hind on an
untroubled sea.

On our arrival, we
heard a report of the
king's own calligrapher
having just died.
What a fortuitous
simultaneity!
Writing for me was a
singular pride.

Snatching a pen and some
pieces of parchment, I
wrote out some verses, both
somber and light.
All were amazed by the
incredibility
of my achievement—an
ape that could write!

Word of my skill reached the
king, who, incredulous,
ordered at once I be
brought to his court,
where I was met by an
oversolicitous
circle of eunuchs much
given to sport.

After a feast, we played
two games of chess (which I
won), and the king, promptly
slapping his knee,
awestruck by something so
extraphenomenal,
summoned his beautiful
daughter to see.

"Father!" the princess cried,
"Why did you call me? Un-
veiled in the sight of a
stranger as well!"
"No one is here but this
anthropomorphical
ape." "No! A king, living
under a spell!"

*With the approach of morning, Scheherazade fell silent, but when the
fourteenth night arrived, she resumed her recital of the kalandar's story:*

Then she recounted my
history: how on a
voyage to Hind I was
shipwrecked, and worse,
how I encountered a
supraluxurious
splendor, a fiend-ravished
girl, and a curse.

Moved by the story, but
heartened to know that his
daughter was learnèd in
mystical lore
(she had been taught by a
nonagenarian
sorceress, child of a
faraway shore),

"Can you," the king asked his
princess, "release our dear
guest from the spell of that
wicked ifrit?"
"Father, I'll try," she said
unterrifiedly,
"though to confront him is
no easy feat."

50

Drawing a circle, she
cryptogrammatically
conjured the evil one,
clutching her breast.
Darkness descended; her
apotropaical
powers would clearly be
put to the test.

Jurjis appeared, and she
sternly accosted him:
"I take no pleasure in
summoning you!"
"Have you forsworn the in-
violability
of our alliance? the
deference due

each to the other?" "It
died with the hideous
curse you imposed on this
excellent man."
Thus did she answer him
undeferentially;
thus their redoubtable
battle began.

Each moved ingeniously,
constantly trying to
gain an advantage with
so much at stake,
using the witchwork of
alterability—
lion and scimitar,
eagle and snake,

black cat and scorpion,
vulture and pomegranate—
ah, the ifrit!—and he
scattered his seed.
Wolf became cock in an
extrafrenetical
effort to swallow them
all. But indeed

one of them landed in
water, becoming a
fish, and the cock, chasing
after, a whale.
On went the fight almost
choreographically,
two fierce antagonists—
which would prevail?

Flaming, they surfaced, and
sparks from the evil one
singed the king's mustache and
burned my left eye.
But the poor princess's
paranormality
couldn't endure; she was
destined to die.

First, though, she called for a
goblet of water, and
praising Allah quickly
lifted my curse.
Then she expounded on
immutability,
speaking the words of a
beautiful verse:

"So it is written (as
willed by Allah!), for the
seed that escaped held the
soul of the djinn.
Though I fought valiantly,
etiologically
once he turned fire he was
certain to win."

Bearing last witness to
God and his Prophet, she
crumbled to cinders. Her
father and I
mourned for a month, and then
Mesopotamia
called to me, outcast and
blind in one eye.

The Ass

> Now I will tell you a
> tale of Rafiki. You've
> heard, I am sure, of that
> masterful thief.
> Are you aware of the
> jiggery-pokery
> by which he cozened a
> simple naif?

*With the approach of morning, Scheherazade fell silent. But when
the three-hundred-and-eightieth night arrived, she resumed:*

> Youssuf the peasant, a
> poor man but honest, lived
> peacefully under the
> laws of the Shah.
> Being, moreover, no
> minimifidian,
> he never questioned the
> ways of Allah.

> Leading his ass through the
> market one day, he was
> seen by Rafiki, that
> cousin of swine.
> "Ah!" sighed the thief with an
> unsatisfiable
> lust for possession, "that
> ass shall be mine."

Slipping the rope from the
jenny, he handed her
off to his fellow in
blackguardly deals,
and with remarkable
inconspicuity
put on the halter and
dug in his heels.

Youssuf, so checked, turned to
see what had happened, and
cried: "An ifrit must have
addled my brain!"
Whereupon, seizing this
epiphenomenal
notion, Rafiki said:
"Let me explain.

"As a young man I would
mistreat my mother and
wallow in other sins
equally crass.
Justly, Allah gave my
egomaniacally
odious soul to an
obstinate ass.

"You then procured me and
treated me badly. The
more that you beat me the
more I would fart,
not understanding the
teleological
ways of Allah, who was
trying my heart.

"Now my dear mother has
prayed for His mercy and
He has released me," the
cunning one said.
Faced with this staggering
inscrutability,
even poor Youssuf was
scratching his head.

Still, he accepted the
loss of his donkey, be-
lieving it must be the
will of Allah,
and he repented those
unjustifiable
beatings and freed the poor
fellow. Voilà![10]

10. It is not for
us to ask why
Scheherazade
would suddenly
speak in French.

Later he spotted his
ass in the market, and
cried out: "You backslider!
Basest of men!
Do you take pride in such
implacability?
Starve if you will—I'll not
buy you again!"

Then pronounced Shahryar:

What a fine story, and
with a delectable
antimetabole
hard to surpass,
for it transfigures an
unsentimentalized
ass to a man and a
man to an ass!

The Historic Fart

Scheherazade having concluded her tale, Shahryar said:
"That is indeed astonishing. It almost made me forget certain
unpleasant duties I have to undertake tomorrow." Answered
Scheherazade: "O King, that tale is nothing compared to the one
about the historic fart." "What is this historic fart? I have never
heard of it." "It is a tale I had intended to tell you tomorrow
night, if I were still alive." So Shahryar said to himself: "I
shall not kill her until I have heard this strange tale." With the
approach of the morning Scheherazade fell silent. But when the
four-hundred-and-sixteenth night had come, she said:

Abu al-Hasan had[11]
abandoned the ways of
the nomad to seek a
luxurious life,
and quickly achieved the
immoderatenesses
of grandeur including
a ravishing wife.

11. Aha!
Amphibrachs yet
again.

But he had been married
for only a year when
Allah took his darling
to infinite grace.
Anon he began his
revitalization
by searching for someone
to wed in her place.

He soon was betrothed to
a damsel as pleasing
as moonshine on water,
and hosted a feast
so lavish it brought him
congratulatory
regard, and assured him
his lot had increased.

The time then arrived for
his entrance unto his
belovèd, the height of
his joy and his pride;
but—curses!—he felt an
intensification
of sudden discomfort
and rumbling inside.

And then an explosion—
a roar and a reek of
such noxious cachet as
to rattle the mind.
Abashed by this worst of
indecorousnesses,
Hasan left his bride and
the city behind.

He raced across deserts
until he arrived at
the sea, then set sail for
the Malabar coast
where word of his shameful
eliminatory
faux pas couldn't get to
the ears of a host.

He quickly found favor,
success, and esteem, and
was even named head of
the sovereign guard.
Protected by rank, his
katalegophobic[12]
distress was forgotten
as last year's foulard.

12. Fearful of
    ridicule.

But he missed his homeland
and wondered if maybe
his earlier shame was
remembered no more.
And were he to make an
extenuatory
appeal to the bride he'd
abandoned before . . .

Returning, the first thing
he heard was a mother
addressing her daughter.
The words cut his heart:
"Today is your birthday,
commemoratively
observed on the day that
Hasan let his fart."

We all perhaps yearn to
be thought of forever,
though lending one's name to
so signal a date
is hardly the path to
immortalization
Hasan would have chosen.
Yet such was his fate.

And still to this day on
disastrous occasions
the people remember
Abu al-Hasan,
whose name has become a
colloquialism
from Qum to Morocco,
Tabriz to Aswan.

When earthquakes demolished
one half of Damascus,
the roar was enough to
tear eardrums apart,
yet still one could hear an
ejaculatory:
"Have mercy, Allah! Did
Hasan blow a fart?"

And those who survived a
tremendous tsunami
that flooded a fourth of
the coastline of Hind
could only describe it
associatively—
"'Twas almost as bad as
Hasan breaking wind!"

The Tale of the Leg of Mutton

Lovely Samira was
too full of passion to
marry just one man and
so married two,
but she had taken such
ideolectual
care for their piety
neither one knew.

Husband Akil was a
pickpocket working where
jugglers and mummers drew
crowds in the park;
husband Haram preferred
invisibility,
practicing theft under
cover of dark.

Such an arrangement went
well until both of them,
on the road, thirsty and
seeking a brew,
met in a hostel, and
complimentarily
started conversing, as
strangers will do.

Boasting about their dear
wives, they discovered that
they were surprisingly
very the same.
Then came a startling in-
explicability:
each had a half leg of
mutton that came

packed in the lunches their
wives had prepared for them,
which, juxtaposed, were ex-
actly aligned.
Though they in ardor were
hyperassiduous,
finding no pleasure in
being unkind,

surely they needed to
question Samira, and
she, understanding the
impasse, was loath,
given her vagary's
unviability,
not to admit that she'd
married them both.

Moved by her tears and her
pleas for forgiveness, they
could not disparage her
marital ruse.
Yet they agreed that for
intrafamilial
peace and the laws of the
faith, she must choose

one husband only. Yet
loving both equally,
how could she possibly
make such a choice?
Musing, and fighting her
nymphomaniacal
nature, at last she dis-
covered her voice:

"Great is Allah, Who will
judge us as we use the
skills He has given us.
You have both shown
you have perfected your
potentiality.
So I will choose to keep
that man alone

"who proves his worthiness
not by his love for me
but by achieving the
cleverest theft."
First then, Akil risked an
ultrafelicitous
sleight-of-hand wondrously
cunning and deft,

not only lifting the
purse of a Jew but con-
vincing the kadi[13] the
purse was his own,
for he'd put in it a
pseudo-Assyrian
ring with an inlay of
hyacinth stone,

13. An Islamic
judge.

slyly conveyed the purse
back to the Jew, and then
charged the poor fellow with
being a thief.
Since the Jew protested
inefficaciously,
"right" was Akil's, for the
Jew only grief.

"Ah, I commend you," cried
husband Haram. You have
set a high standard. But
meet me tonight,
when I will show you an
extraprofessional
feat of *my* artistry,
arch and forthright.

"Come to the sultan's east
garden, and witness how
I shall put over a
trick to top yours.
Thus we'll determine (with
nonarbitrariness)
which of our talents our
wife most adores."

*With the approach of morning, Scheherazade fell silent, but when
the seven-hundred-and-eighty-eighth night arrived, she resumed:*

Midnight. Haram led the
dumbstruck Akil to the
room where the sultan him-
self was asleep,
tended by one who was
unconscientiously
fanning his master while
drifting in deep,

khat-induced lethargy.
Quickly Haram moved to
bind up and gag him and
then took his stead,
fanning the sultan quite
self-satisfiedly.
Sensing him stir, Haram
quietly said,

mocking the voice of the
manhandled menial:
"O King of Time, shall I
tell you a tale?"
"Certainly," answered the
semipercipient
sultan. Haram then set
out to regale

himself and his ruler: "There
once was a thief by the
name of Haram . . ." and went
on to reveal
(truth to tell, just a bit
antagonistically)
what had gone on between
him and Akil—

how dear Samira had
married the two of them,
how she intended to
right her disgrace,
challenging each to a
multidimensional
exploit to prove himself
worth her embrace,

how the pickpocket had
fleeced a poor Jew, and the
robber had entered the
sultan's own room,
bound up his servant, and
egocentristically
told his own story and
waits for his doom.

"Which of the two was more
clever, O Sultan?" The
sultan averred as his
eyes gently closed,
"Surely that masterful
prodigiosity
who had his sport while the
sultan reposed."

Rising, Haram flashed a
grin at Akil, and the
two left the palace, not
saying a word.
Later that morning, the
indelibility
of the impression of
what had occurred

troubled the sultan un-
til he discovered his
servant trussed up, and he
realized then
he had been victimized
(semihypnotically?)
in his own room by the
slyest of men.

Rather than seething with
anger, he pardoned the
clever one, adding a
purseful of gold,
thereby surpassing the
profitability
of Akil's pickings by
two hundredfold.

Further to honor such
outright audacity,
he made Haram the realm's
chief of police.
Oh, and Samira chose
meritocratically,
keeping Haram. May Al-
lah grant them peace.

The Invitation to Universal Peace

Then said Scheherazade:

> Voice-of-the-Dawn, who was
> known for his wisdom, one
> morning was walking when
> suddenly—Fox!—
> certainly one of those
> aleatorical
> meetings not pleasing to
> wandering cocks.

> Frantically flapping, he
> managed a tentative
> refuge on top of a
> rotten old fence,
> where he probed possible
> extricability
> from a dilemma so
> parlously tense.

With the approach of morning, Scheherazade fell silent. But when
the seven-hundred-and-ninety-sixth night had come, she resumed:

> "Peace be upon you, my
> brother," said Fox. When the
> cock answered nothing, he
> added, "You choose
> not to address me. Your
> inaffability
> hurts, for I come but to
> bring you good news.

"Lion and Eagle have
issued an edict that
all of the beasts, whether
feathered or furred,
live in benevolent
amiability.
I've been appointed to
carry the word.

"Tiger and antelope,
jackal and basilisk,
hawk and hyena and
pigeon and dove—
all shall inhabit a
paradisiacal
garden of peace and of
brotherly love.

"Old animosities
must be forgotten and
any recidivist
will be condemned."
Fox's rhetorical
armamentarium
being depleted, his
fancy was stemmed.

Still hearing nothing, he
snapped, "And unless you em-
brace me, the fiat will
not be fulfilled.
Peace will become the new
universality
even if half of us
have to be killed."

During these palpable
illogicalities
Voice-of-the-Dawn was too
anxious to crow.
His mind was otherwise,
preoccupiedly
mulling a method to
outfox his foe.

"Pardon, my friend. I meant
no impoliteness, but
as you were talking," he
answered at last,
"I was distraught by some
unspecifiable
something approaching and
coming on fast."

"Is it a greyhound?" asked
Fox with a tremor. "It
might be . . . I think so . . . a
beast of that breed."
"That's disconcerting, for
incomprehensibly
he wasn't thought of when
peace was decreed.

"Brother, I leave you. That
pimp of a greyhound can
never be trusted." With
that he was gone.
Mocking the fox's own
pseudo-sincerity
proved the salvation of
Voice-of-the-Dawn.

Then pronounced Shahryar:

> Ah, the unspeakable
> ideological
> balderdash only the
> shameless commit!
> Praise to Allah when such
> self-contradictory
> cunning is routed by
> wisdom and wit!

The Tale of the First Captain

Then Scheherazade told of a sultan of Egypt who especially loved and honored storytellers. He called together his captains of police and bade them each tell a story. Here is the tale told by the first captain:

Having good reason to
savor my greatness (the
people bow meekly when-
ever I pass),
I take delight in my
unpopularity,
feared as I am by each
son of an ass.

One day, patrolling, I
slipped up an alley and
sat by a wall for a
bit of a nap.
Suddenly (could it be
unaccidentally?)
something fell heavily
into my lap.

Mercy! A purse with a
hundred dinars! I saw
no one about. With a
quick by-your-leave
asked of Allah and no
circumlocutional
wherefores, I buried the
purse in my sleeve.

Next day, returning, I
slyly pretended to
sleep, surreptitiously
keeping close watch,
counting, you see, on the
infinitesimal
odds of—but someone was
groping my crotch!

Startled, I seized what I
hardly expected, a
damsel's bejeweled and
fairy-like hand.
"Sweet one," I ventured, not
undiplomatically,
"tell me your wish; I am
yours to command."

"Follow me, Captain, if
you wish an answer." She
led me up alleys I'd
never patrolled.
Thinking to please her, I
unhesitatingly
took out my zabb.[14] She said: 14. I trust no
"Won't he catch cold?   translation is
                                         needed for this.

"Put him away." "But if
he doesn't tempt you, then
why did you give me the
purse, and behave
so unbecomingly?"
Undisconcertedly
smiling, she said, "It's not
you that I crave.

"I am a girl who is
madly in love with a
beautiful woman, as
she is with me.
Sadly, however, her
extracensorious
father the kadi will
not let us be.

"He has forbidden our
promise of passion (that
gnarly old miser!), and
keeps us apart.
Help us inhabit that
supraerogenous
joy which alone can bring
peace to my heart."

Puzzled by this, I thought,
"Girls will be boys?" So I
tactfully asked (for I
wanted to know,
not being noted for
incuriosity),
"What kind of love has a
doe for a doe?"

*As morning approached, Scheherazade discreetly fell silent, but when the nine-
hundred-and-thirty-eighth night had come, she continued with the girl's words:*

"Love is a mystery
few can elucidate;
it is enough that you
help with my ruse.
Since it is legal, your
nonculpability's
never in doubt; you have
nothing to lose.

"Dressing tonight in my
finest array, I'll a-
wait your patrol by the
kadi's abode.
When they arrive, I'll be
unrecognizably
veiled, and pretend to be
lost in the road.

"This is the story I'll
tell to beguile them: that
I was out shopping and
stayed out too late,
which quite unsafely and
undignifiedly
left me locked out at the
citadel gate.

"Itching to help me, they'll
ask you to summon the
kadi and tell him to
take care of me."
"Sweet one," as I again
hypocoristically
called her, "your cleverness
wins you your plea."

All went as planned, and the
kadi agreed that his
daughter could welcome her
in for the night.
I was still lost in my
unapprehendingness . . .
two gazelles romping in
wanton delight?

When I arrived at the
kadi's next morning, a
fury accosted me,
shouting, "You louse!"
Why was I met with such
inimicality?
"Scoundrel! You planted a
thief in my house!

"Blessèd Allah, she has
stolen a belt with six
hundred dinars! It will
cost you your head!"
(He was a judge, and spoke
jurisprudentially!)
"Give me a few days to
find her," I pled.

Though he agreed, I had
no way of finding her.
Downcast, I took to my
bed for three days.
Was such a robbery's
unsolvability
destined to settle my
venial ways?

On my way back to the
kadi's, I saw in a
window my sweet one, the
cause of my grief!
"Wretch!" I yelled up at her
deprecatorily,
"why have you made me the
dog of a thief?"

Calling me up to her,
she reassured me, and
ushered me into a
fabulous room
bursting with rubies and
unclassifiable
treasure. "Despite what you
seem to assume,

"why would I steal? I made
off with the money in
hopes the old miser would
die of a stroke.
You needn't fear; I've a
superingenious
scheme to cast him as the
butt of the joke.

"Go to the kadi and
tell him I never went
out of his house, but am
hidden away.
Though he will challenge the
nonsensicality
of your hypothesis,
do as I say:

"Search, and while doing so
go to the kitchen, and
there you'll discover a
sinister sight—
my bloody clothing, a
frightened-to-death-ative[15]
horror. The kadi might
well die of fright,

15. Cf. "the
people screamed
all sorts o'
frightened-to-
death-ativeness"
attributed to Davy
Crockett, from his
"autobiography," c.
1833.

"and if he doesn't, at
least he'll do anything
just to keep secret what
happened to me.
Yet if Allah wills the
unworkability
of our deception, then
so it shall be."

"If we succeed, will you
marry me, sweetest one,
so that my itch can be
roundly assuaged?"
Smiling, she cited its
unfeasibility:
"Have you forgotten my
heart is engaged?"

At this point Scheherazade saw the approach of morning and discreetly fell silent,
but when the nine-hundred-and-thirty-ninth night had come, she continued:

When I returned to the
kadi and offered my
theory, he blithered some
feckless tirade
as with conspicuous
inexpeditiousness
I toured his premises—
what a charade!

While I was searching, I
glimpsed her belovèd, and
knew how a rose might be
drawn to a rose.
Finally, shouting an
overdemonstrative
"Ha!" I uncovered the
bundle of clothes.

78

Swooning, the terrified
kadi paid dear for my
silence, and died soon there-
after, the cur.
Sweet one, I hear, lives in
cohabitational
bliss with her jonquil. My
blessing on her.

III. REYNARD THE FOX

Reynard the Fox

Whitsun: the season for
Nobel the lion to
summon his subjects both
sinners and saints—
time for the annual
judicatorial
omnium gatherum
of their complaints.

This year like all years the
special tribunal was
marked from the outset by
choleric flocks
forming a chorus of
animadversionists
slinging their charges at
Reynard the fox.

There was a litany
of the nefarious
ways he behaved any
number of times.
What a rich trove for a
praxeological
study describing the
nature of crimes!

Isegrim[16] outlined how
Reynard, the caitiff, had
blinded his pups and in-
sulted his wife,
and just that morning had
sociopathically
beaten poor Lampe[17] half
out of his life.

16. The wolf.

17. The hare.

Reynard of course was not
present as Isegrim
told with great anguish his
sorrowful tale.
Grimbart[18] pled various
mitigabilities,
arguing only that
justice prevail:

18. The badger,
Reynard's nephew.

"Isegrim partnered with
Reynard in thieving, but
viciously cheated him
out of his share,
leaving him nothing but
unappetizingly
maggoty fish heads—and
as for the hare . . .

"Well, my good uncle was
merely instructing the
creature in psalmody
and it appears
sometimes his frustrating
duncical-headedness
richly deserved a light
box on the ears.

"All of these charges do
wrong to my uncle, for
ever since general
peace was declared,
he's led the life of a
Premonstratensian,[19]
fasting and praying, and
sparingly laired."

19. Member of
a religious order
founded by St.
Norbert in 1120,
characterized by
great austerity.

Nobel was taken with
Grimbart's avowal, when
Henning came suddenly
into the room,
shouting of horrors most
amphitheatrically.
Was the fox finally
facing his doom?

"All my brood dead, and my
favorite hen but a
mangle . . . because of your
edict,[20] my king!
We let our guard down, thus
oxymoronically
letting that reprobate
do such a thing!"

20. I.e., the declaration of universal peace.

Nobel was outraged, and
spoke with resolve as the
harsh allegations con-
tinued to mount:
"This exhibition of
anticivility
angers us. Let him be
brought to account."

Bruin was chosen to
fetch him to court, but was
warned to beware of the
wiles of the fox.
Braving Malterra's im-
penetrability,
tangles of briers and
marshes and rocks,

weary and wounded and
thoroughly waterlogged,
Bruin at last came to
Reynard's retreat.
Reynard beguilingly,
self-deprecatingly,
could offer nothing but
honey to eat.

Bruin, forgetting his
mission, accepted with
relish. Said Reynard: "I
know of a tree
not very far from here
overabundantly
flowing with honey; come
with me and see."

At the tree Bruin had
greedily thrust both his
snout and his paws in the
honey when snapped
(with some assistance) a
disadvantageously
atrophied limb, and poor
Bruin was trapped.

21. The cat.

Told of this travesty,
Nobel charged Hintze[21] to
go to Malterra, and
no more delay—
Reynard must come to the
antemeridian
session at court on the
very next day.

Reynard bid welcome to
Hintze, and promised to
go on the morrow with
him to the court,
then diabolically,
premeditatedly
asked if he'd like to go
mousing for sport.

Hintze agreeing, they
made for a barn which had
not only mice but a
dangerous snare
meant to catch fox, but its
nonselectivity
sprang just as quickly at
cats unaware.

Nobel, when told of this
second fiasco, was
livid: "I swear that I'll
get him! Amen."
Grimbart, without any
sentimentality,
came to his uncle's de-
fense yet again,

pleading that Bruin and
Hintze were caught not by
Reynard's deceit but by
faults of their own.
Yet he respectfully,
impertinaciously,
promised to bring him to
court to atone.

He reached Malterra, and
frankly told Reynard the
mood of the king and his
latest command.
"I must obey," said the
paterfamilias,
"now, before everything
gets out of hand."

He bid adieu to his
wife and his little ones,
wondering what he might
say to the king,
mulling and weighing the
serviceability
of each conceivable
case he might bring.

As they were walking, he
felt a strong impulse to
boast of his cunning both
current and past.
All the magnificent
happy-go-luckiness
toward his wrongdoing left
Grimbart aghast.

Once he'd tied Isegrim's
tail to a bell rope; the
clamor he caused got him
drubbed by the folks.
Reynard just chuckled. What
incurability
in this addiction to
practical jokes!

Still, the good nephew, who
served as confessor, for-
gave him, no matter how
cruel the trick,
since as a penance he'd
ritualistically
flog his own back and leap
over the stick.

Maybe contrition was
suffered too easily—
unpenitentially,
hardly for real—
since he relapsed into
unscrupulosity
when he caught sight of some
chickens to steal.

Grimbart, however, by
keeping an eye on him,
got him to court, where the
king and his lords
waited with all of the
organizational
pomp such a circumstance
always affords.

Reynard, unruffled, with
riveting eloquence,
lauded himself as a
most loyal liege:
"Surely my conduct is
noncontroversial;
who dares to question my
peerless prestige?"

Nobel reminded him
that he had treated both
Henning and Hintze in
terrible ways.
Others accused him of
mulierosity,[22]
thievery, carnage, and
fostering frays.

22. Inordinate lust for married women or women of low character.

Reynard's fine rhetoric
proved ineffective, and
he was found guilty. No
mercy; instead,
council decreed with no
huggery-muggery,
"Let him be hanged by the
neck until dead."

Many were thrilled by the
verdict and hurried to
witness the hanging, while
Reynard himself,
faced with this seeming in-
superability,
sought for a way to get
out of this delf.[23]

23. A pit or excavation; here obviously one of Reynard's own digging.

Why not beg leave for a
public confession, a
chance to explain why his
life had gone wrong?
"Isegrim counseled me
anticommunally,
'Prey on the powerless,
flatter the strong'—

"taught me the 'virtue' of
greed, and then cheated me,
leaving me destitute.
Oh, he was cold!
I would have starved had not
extrafortuitous
circumstance led me to
. . . gold."

Reynard knew instantly
he'd played it perfectly;
Nobel perked up at this
spurious news,
born of the dazzling in-
imitability
of his evasions—a
masterly ruse.

"I," he continued, "had
learned that my father was
plotting with Isegrim
(and I surmise
Bruin and Hintze were
co-insurrectionists)—
planning to flummox the
king's enterprise.

"For such a purpose, my
father had hoarded a
treasure in gold to take
care of the cost.
I found the prospect most
unentertainable.
Had they succeeded, what
might have been lost?"

Then he went on to tell
(self-aggrandizingly
building his story on
lie upon lie)
how he'd prevented the
periclitational[24]
scheme by removing the
gold on the sly.

24. Periclitation:
"The action
of exposing or
condition of
being exposed
to peril: peril,
danger, hazard,
jeopardy."—OED.

"That cost me dearly, for
father, distraught by the
loss of his treasure (its
loss, don't you see,
rendered their stratagem
unexecutable),
strung himself up from an
apricot tree."

As he had figured, that
won the queen's sympathy.
Helpful, but what about
Nobel? Well, he
thought about waging a
counterinsurgency . . .
and about gold, and an-
nounced a decree

for the arrest of the
malcontents—Isegrim,
Bruin, and Hintze—and,
urged by his wife,
offered to pardon the
polyrecidivist . . .
if he would barter the
gold for his life.

Reynard accepted, of
course, and told Nobel just
where he could locate the
gold in the fen,
though with a curious
nonspecificity
which left the king at a
loss yet again.

Puffing his pardon, the
fox asked the hare to Mal-
terra for dinner, if
he wouldn't mind.
Too well attuned to the
amphibological
terms of the overture,
Lampe declined.

Nobel soon realized
there was no treasure, and
summoned poor Reynard to
answer at law.
May be our hero knew
premonitorily
this would at last be the
very last straw.

He was aware that the
king had acquitted the
trio that he had so
falsely accused.
Must he accept the un-
pardonability
of the chicanery
he'd so abused?

Wondering what he might
possibly say in his
pending defense, he be-
gan to rehearse:
Nobel's a master of
unethicality;
priests are all sinners. Am
I any worse?

I've done your majesty's
bidding most faithfully,
served your cause loyally
(so he would plead),
and I was steadfastly
imparsimonious,
sharing my booty with
others in need.

Confident that he could
quit himself quickly, he
made his appearance and
knelt to the king.
Artfully humble, in
non-adversarial
tones, he proceeded to
risk everything.

Nobel forestalled the in-
terminability
of his incredible
lies to the court,
citing their wearisome
irrisibility.
Clearly the king was in
no mood for sport.

Seeing how things were pro-
ceeding against him, he
bowed to his monarch, and
kissing the rod,
begged the tradition of
extrapolitical
combat of right, leaving
judgment to God.

He would meet Isegrim,
one-on-one combat, the
winner found guiltless by
triumph *per se.*
Nobel agreed, and the
caconomasian[25]
contest was set for the
following day.

25. Badly named;
misnamed.

Isegrim battled him
mightily, fiercely, but
Reynard prevailed, and the
king in reward
not only pardoned him
unprejudicially,
but within minutes had
named him a lord.

Everyone fawned on their
erstwhile tormentor who'd
won the king's favor and
been newly earled.
Are we surprised by their
temperamentality?
Isn't that always the
way of the world?

Reynard, however, when
offered preferment and
sanction at court, thought it
best to forbear,
being essentially
antiestablishment:
"I miss Malterra; I'd
rather be there."

———

> To wisdom let all men
> Quickly apply them, and flee what is evil, and reverence virtue.
> This is the end and aim of the song, and in it the poet
> Fable and truth hath mixed, whereby the good from the evil
> Ye may discern, and wisdom esteem; and thereby the buyers
> Of this book in the ways of the world may be daily instructed.
> For it was created of old, and will ever remain so.
> Thus is our poem of Reineke's deeds and character ended.
> May God bring us all to eternal happiness.
> Amen!

Notes

The double dactyl, or "Higgledy-piggledy" (so called because originally the first line consisted of such a nonsense term), was created by Paul Pascal and Anthony Hecht. It made its first public appearance in *Esquire* in June 1966, and later that year in a collection of such verses, *Jiggery Pokery,* edited by Hecht and John Hollander. Each double dactyl was a discrete verse and required eight lines of dactylic dimeter (DA da da DA da da), with truncated fourth and eighth lines rhyming; the second line was a proper name (Emily Dickinson, Theodore Roosevelt, etc.), and one line in the second quatrain, usually the sixth, consisted of a single didactylic word.

I have taken a few liberties with the form in adapting it to these narratives, forgoing nonsensicality in the opening line and generally dispensing with proper names in the second, but have consistently made the sixth line a single word. There is an obvious metrical variation, of course, in those verses (e.g., "The Taming of the Shrew") written in amphibrachs (da DA da da DA da) rather than dactyls.

The source for the tales adapted from the Arabian Nights is *The Book of the Thousand Nights and One Night,* translated by Powys Mathers from the French of J.C. Mardrus (New York, NY: St. Martin's, 1972), respectively I, 72–89; II, 384–85; III, 221–23; III, 483–88; III, 515–18; IV, 340–50.

Reynard (or Reineke) the fox has been a traditional character in Northern European folklore for centuries, and written versions of his adventures have appeared in Latin, French, German, and Dutch since the mid-twelfth century. William Caxton printed the first English version, translated from the Dutch, in 1481, and Goethe wrote his long poem *Reineke Fuchs* in 1794. For this version, I have worked mostly from H.A. Guerber's "Reynard the Fox" in his *Legends of the Middle Ages* (New York, NY: American Book Co., 1896). The epilogue is translated from Goethe's *Reineke Fuchs.*

Jan D. Hodge grew up in a letterpress printing shop in small town Michigan, and received his BA and MA degrees from the University of Michigan and his PhD from the University of New Mexico, where he wrote his dissertation on Charles Dickens. He taught at Rockford (Illinois) College and at Morningside College in Sioux City, Iowa.

His poems have appeared in many print and online journals and anthologies, and his book *Taking Shape,* a collection of *carmina figurata,* was published in 2015 by Able Muse Press.

ALSO FROM ABLE MUSE PRESS

William Baer, *Times Square and Other Stories*

Melissa Balmain, *Walking in on People – Poems*

Ben Berman, *Figuring in the Figure – Poems*

Ben Berman, *Strange Borderlands – Poems*

Michael Cantor,
　Life in the Second Circle – Poems

Catherine Chandler, *Lines of Flight – Poems*

William Conelly, *Uncontested Grounds – Poems*

Maryann Corbett,
　Credo for the Checkout Line in Winter – Poems

John Philip Drury, *Sea Level Rising – Poems*

D.R. Goodman, *Greed: A Confession – Poems*

Margaret Ann Griffiths,
　Grasshopper – The Poetry of M A Griffiths

Katie Hartsock, *Bed of Impatiens – Poems*

Elise Hempel, *Second Rain – Poems*

Jan D. Hodge, *Taking Shape – carmina figurata*

Ellen Kaufman, *House Music – Poems*

Emily Leithauser, *The Borrowed World – Poems*

Carol Light, *Heaven from Steam – Poems*

April Lindner,
　This Bed Our Bodies Shaped – Poems

Martin McGovern, *Bad Fame – Poems*

Jeredith Merrin, *Cup – Poems*

Richard Newman,
　All the Wasted Beauty of the World – Poems

Alfred Nicol, *Animal Psalms – Poems*

Frank Osen, *Virtue, Big as Sin – Poems*

Alexander Pepple (Editor),
　Able Muse Anthology

Alexander Pepple (Editor),
　Able Muse – a review of poetry, prose & art
　(semiannual issues, Winter 2010 onward)

James Pollock, *Sailing to Babylon – Poems*

Aaron Poochigian, *The Cosmic Purr – Poems*

John Ridland,
　Sir Gawain and the Green Knight –
　Translation

Stephen Scaer, *Pumpkin Chucking – Poems*

Hollis Seamon, *Corporeality – Stories*

Carrie Shipers, *Cause for Concern – Poems*

Matthew Buckley Smith,
　Dirge for an Imaginary World – Poems

Barbara Ellen Sorensen,
　Compositions of the Dead Playing Flutes –
　Poems

Wendy Videlock,
　Slingshots and Love Plums – Poems

Wendy Videlock,
　The Dark Gnu and Other Poems

Wendy Videlock, *Nevertheless – Poems*

Richard Wakefield, *A Vertical Mile – Poems*

Gail White, *Asperity Street – Poems*

Chelsea Woodard, *Vellum – Poems*

www.ablemusepress.com

www.ingramcontent.com/pod-product-compliance
Lightning Source LLC
Chambersburg PA
CBHW021407090426
42742CB00009B/1040